The Looking Glass

Photographs by Via Wynroth

A book is always a long journey. For their encouragement and support, my appreciation to Cornell Capa, Mrs. Jolan Glück, and Judith Horstman.

International Standard Book Number 0-87100-141-1

Library of Congress Catalog Card Number 77-93625

Book Design by John O'Mara
Typeset in Palatino
Printed in Quadradot Lithography by Morgan Press, Inc.

Distributed by
Morgan & Morgan, Inc.
145 Palisade Street
Dobbs Ferry, New York 10522

THE LOOKING GLASS

Why, you may ask, dear peruser, a book? I, too, have asked and re-asked the question. Somehow in this final setting, it allows me to bid farewell to the people I worked with for two and a half years as a social worker.

These photographs were taken in a 'shelter-care' home and at its sister nursing home.

Reality has many faces and what remains are evocations—memories that scream of isolation and long days of silence.

If the shadows in Plato's cave can reveal anything, it is that these images express an unalienable bond between myself and other human beings.

I dedicate this book to my mother and to the people who allowed me to see my own reflection in the looking glass.

O*nce there was a king who sought the advice of a wise man.*

He said: Every night when I go to sleep I dream I am a butterfly. When I awake in the morning, all day I think I am a king.

Can you tell me which is the reality?

Am I a king dreaming he is a butterfly or a butterfly dreaming he is a king?

parable

Via: I can't hear you . . . you're dreaming, Charles.

Charles: Yeah, I dream . . . all the time. Different things I dream about. One fellow says, why don't you just . . . dream that you were, you know. . . somebody. And you wanted to be just like every other, maybe ordinary citizen. And such things as having a home, and acting as normally, functioning normally. . . . as most individuals, persons do. . .

Mamie

Madeline

Shirley

So I landed up there. (State Hospital) And I said, 'How do I get out of here?' They said, 'Well, your mother can take you out when she's ready but you have to stay here awhile.'

But it was a long while . . . It was 28 years.

So, I just thought, well, this is my home. I have to work myself out, be good and work myself out. So that's what I had to do all those years. . .

I dream an awful lot. I don't know what makes that. Once, I dreamed my mother was coming to take me home. When I woke up the next day, I thought, oh gosh, am I dreaming that?

Fanny

Charles

Mary

Kiyo

Rose

Mary

I remember her psychiatrist and some of us discussing her. We really wondered where Gretchen's place was because she'd keep wandering away from the home. She was a wanderer, she'd go off for days.

I don't know how many times the home sent her money to return because she was a favorite. I remember the last time, she got way up north some place. There was a debate. We were willing to have her back but the hospital said she was dangerous to herself. They committed her.

Some people thought she should be locked up in jail but all she wanted to do was just wander around.

social worker

Charles

Frank

I'm lying here looking at the four walls thinking a son has to pass away, a husband as young as him passed away...

I have nothing to thank God for. Even though I do go to Mass every week, I feel God hasn't been, wasn't good to me. Maybe he doesn't like me for some reason, I don't know...

All I want to do is die and go to heaven.

Estelle

Bernice

William

There really is a God! And He's exactly like the Bible describes Him. He's white and He shines like the sun, only He's like a sheet. . . holy, you know. He just laughed at me when I asked Him, why?

Tammy

Sylvia

Sara and Mary

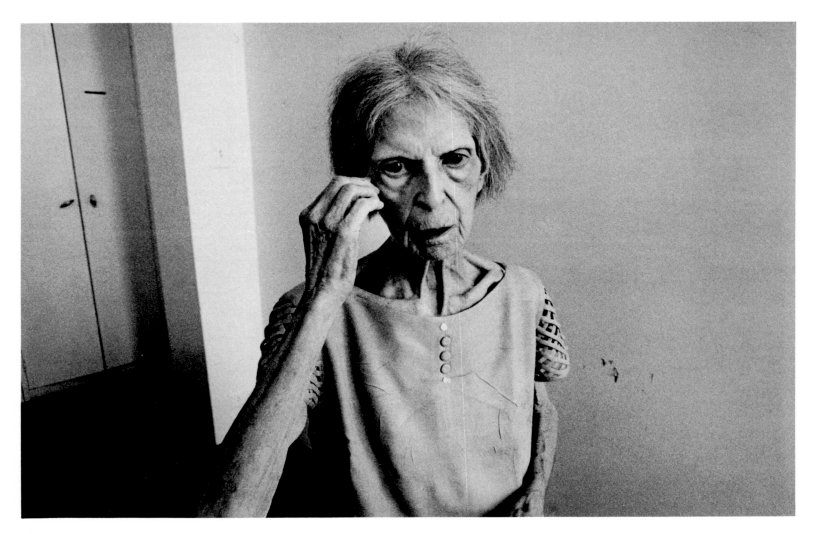

Catherine

It's three years now we've been married since we left the home. If we'd gone out alone, we'd probably have been awfully lonely, but together we're able to handle it. You know, if Alex went out and got an apartment alone and I went out and got an apartment alone, we'd be two lonely people. You know what I mean? It's a funny way to put it, but. . .

Josephine

Alex and Josephine

Marie and Gilbert

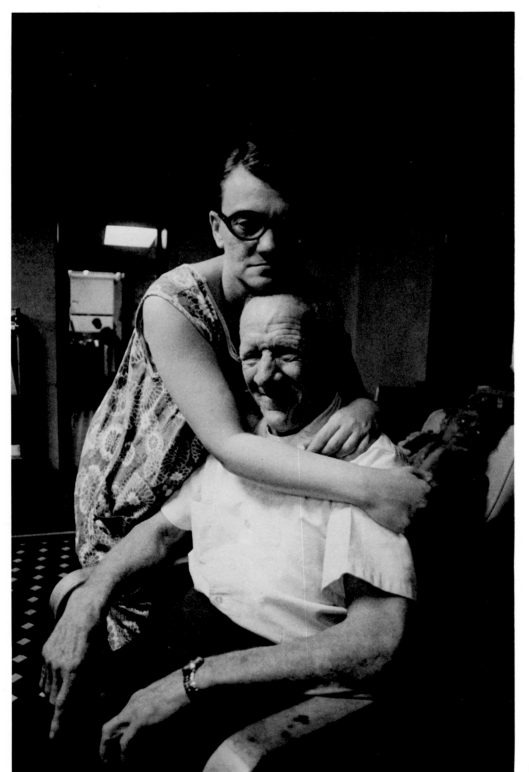

Sally and Henry

Tony

I'm 94. Now, some say I'm foolish. The Father comes for Mass every morning during the week and I wash and iron everything.

I just want to be useful. I'm used to working and I think you should make use of your talents. I don't want to be a lady of leisure.

Mary, keeper of the chapel

Barbara

Look where I am! It's one of the last places. We talk about sickness. When I was born, I had epilepsy, then I got malaria, then I had syphilis, then I got TB, then I had that accident. . . . all those broken bones . . . two lungs collapsed. I am a wreck! (laughs) Just name it, I had it.

But in some way, it's alright. Here I am. Always as a young boy, I taste the nice things. I have the opportunity for love, you know, for pleasure, to travel, to experience. I tasted of everything and I am so glad for it.

I don't mind so much the sickness because after the sickness, it is a new day, you know with all the trimmings. Life is a beautiful thing. I get along with life.

Victor

Daniel

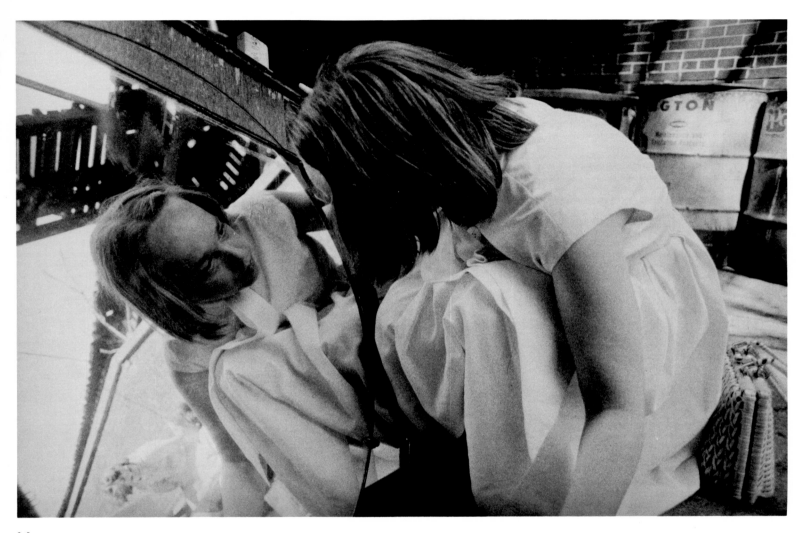

Mary